In A Balcony by Robert Browning

Robert Browning is one of the most significant Victorian Poets and, of course, English Poetry.

Much of his reputation is based upon his mastery of the dramatic monologue although his talents encompassed verse plays and even a well-regarded essay on Shelley during a long and prolific career.

He was born on May 7th, 1812 in Walmouth, London. Much of his education was home based and Browning was an eclectic and studious student, learning several languages and much else across a myriad of subjects, interests and passions.

Browning's early career began promisingly. The fragment from his intended long poem Pauline brought him to the attention of Dante Gabriel Rossetti, and was followed by Paracelsus, which was praised by both William Wordsworth and Charles Dickens. In 1840 the difficult Sordello, which was seen as willfully obscure, brought his career almost to a standstill.

Despite these artistic and professional difficulties his personal life was about to become immensely fulfilling. He began a relationship with, and then married, the older and better known Elizabeth Barrett. This new foundation served to energise his writings, his life and his career.

During their time in Italy they both wrote much of their best work. With her untimely death in 1861 he returned to London and thereafter began several further major projects.

The collection Dramatis Personae (1864) and the book-length epic poem The Ring and the Book (1868-69) were published and well received; his reputation as a venerated English poet now assured.

Robert Browning died in Venice on December 12th, 1889.

Index of Contents
PERSONS
IN A BALCONY
ROBERT BROWNING – A SHORT BIOGRAPHY
ROBERT BROWNING – A CONCISE BIBLIOGRAPHY

Written in 1853, partly at Bagni di Lucca, partly at Rome. It was included in the original series of Men and Women and there divided into three parts.

PERSONS

NORBERT
CONSTANCE
THE QUEEN

CONSTANCE and **NORBERT**.

NORBERT
Now!

CONSTANCE
Not now!

NORBERT
Give me them again, those hands:
Put them upon my forehead, how it throbs!
Press them before my eyes, the fire comes through!
You cruellest, you dearest in the world,
Let me! The Queen must grant whate'er I ask—
How can I gain you and not ask the Queen?
There she stays waiting for me, here stand you;
Some time or other this was to be asked;
Now is the one time—what I ask, I gain:
Let me ask now, Love!

CONSTANCE
Do, and ruin us!

NORBERT
Let it be now, Love! All my soul breaks forth.
How I do love you! Give my love its way!
A man can have but one life and one death,
One heaven, one hell. Let me fulfil my fate—
Grant me my heaven now! Let me know you mine,
Prove you mine, write my name upon your brow,
Hold you and have you, and then die away,
If God please, with completion in my soul!

CONSTANCE
I am not yours then? How content this man!
I am not his—who change into himself,
Have passed into his heart and beat its beats,
Who give my hands to him, my eyes, my hair,
Give all that was of me away to him—
So well, that now, my spirit turned his own,
Takes part with him against the woman here,
Bids him not stumble at so mere a straw
As caring that the world be cognizant

How he loves her and how she worships him.
You have this woman, not as yet that world.
Go on, I bid, nor stop to care for me
By saving what I cease to care about,
The courtly name and pride of circumstance—
The name you 'll pick up and be cumbered with
Just for the poor parade's sake, nothing more;
Just that the world may slip from under you—
Just that the world may cry, "So much for him—
The man predestined to the heap of crowns:
There goes his chance of winning one, at least!"

NORBERT
The world!

CONSTANCE
You love it! Love me quite as well,
And see if I shall pray for this in vain!
Why must you ponder what it knows or thinks?

NORBERT
You pray for—what, in vain?

CONSTANCE
Oh my heart's heart,
How I do love you, Norbert! That is right:
But listen, or I take my hands away!
You say, "let it be now:" you would go now
And tell the Queen, perhaps six steps from us,
You love me—so you do, thank God!

NORBERT
Thank God!

CONSTANCE
Yes, Norbert,—but you fain would tell your love,
And, what succeeds the telling, ask of her
My hand. Now take this rose and look at it,
Listening to me. You are the minister,
The Queen's first favorite, nor without a cause.
To-night completes your wonderful year's-work
(This palace-feast is held to celebrate)
Made memorable by her life's success,
The junction of two crowns, on her sole head,
Her house had only dreamed of anciently:
That this mere dream is grown a stable truth,
To-night's feast makes authentic. Whose the praise?
Whose genius, patience, energy, achieved

What turned the many heads and broke the hearts?
You are the fate, your minute 's in the heaven.
Next comes the Queen's turn. "Name your own reward!"
With leave to clench the past, chain the to-come,
Put out an arm and touch and take the sun
And fix it ever full-faced on your earth,
Possess yourself supremely of her life,—
You choose the single thing she will not grant;
Nay, very declaration of which choice
Will turn the scale and neutralize your work:
At best she will forgive you, if she can.
You think I 'll let you choose—her cousin's hand?

NORBERT
Wait. First, do you retain your old belief
The Queen is generous,—nay, is just?

CONSTANCE
There, there!
So men make women love them, while they know
No more of women's hearts than ... look you here,
You that are just and generous beside.
Make it your own case! For example now,
I 'll say—I let you kiss me, hold my hands—
Why? do you know why? I 'll instruct you, then—
The kiss, because you have a name at court;
This hand and this, that you may shut in each
A jewel, if you please to pick up such.
That 's horrible? Apply it to the Queen—
Suppose I am the Queen to whom you speak.
"I was a nameless man; you needed me:
Why did I proffer yon my aid? there stood
A certain pretty cousin at your side.
Why did I make such common cause with you?
Access to her had not been easy else.
You give my labor here abundant praise?
'Faith, labor, which she overlooked, grew play.
How shall your gratitude discharge itself?
Give me her hand!"

NORBERT
And still I urge the same.
Is the Queen just? just—generous or no!

CONSTANCE
Yes, just. You love a rose: no harm in that:
But was it for the rose's sake or mine
You put it in your bosom? mine, you said—

Then, mine you still must say or else be false.
You told the Queen you served her for herself;
If so, to serve her was to serve yourself,
She thinks, for all your unbelieving face!
I know her. In the hall, six steps from us,
One sees the twenty pictures: there 's a life
Better than life, and yet no life at all.
Conceive her born in such a magic dome,
Pictures all round her! why, she sees the world,
Can recognize its given things and facts,
The fight of giants or the feast of gods,
Sages in senate, beauties at the bath,
Chases and battles, the whole earth's display,
Landscape and sea-piece, down to flowers and fruit—
And who shall question that she knows them all,
In better semblance than the things outside?
Yet bring into the silent gallery
Some live thing to contrast in breath and blood,
Some lion, with the painted lion there—
You think she 'll understand composedly?
—Say, "that 's his fellow in the hunting-piece
Yonder, I 've turned to praise a hundred times?"
Not so. Her knowledge of our actual earth,
Its hopes and fears, concerns and sympathies,
Must be too far, too mediate, too unreal.
The real exists for us outside, not her:
How should it, with that life in these four walls,
That father and that mother, first to last
No father and no mother—friends, a heap,
Lovers, no lack—a husband in due time,
And every one of them alike a lie!
Things painted by a Rubens out of naught
Into what kindness, friendship, love should be;
All better, all more grandiose than the life,
Only no life; mere cloth and surface-paint,
You feel, while you admire. How should she feel?
Yet now that she has stood thus fifty years
The sole spectator in that gallery,
You think to bring this warm real struggling love
In to her of a sudden, and suppose
She 'll keep her state untroubled? Here 's the truth—
She 'll apprehend truth's value at a glance,
Prefer it to the pictured loyalty?
You only have to say, "So men are made,
For this they act; the thing has many names,
But this the right one: and now, Queen, be just!"
Your life slips back; you lose her at the word:
You do not even for amends gain me.

He will not understand! oh, Norbert, Norbert,
Do you not understand?

NORBERT
The Queen 's the Queen,
I am myself—no picture, but alive
In every nerve and every muscle, here
At the palace-window o'er the people's street,
As she in the gallery where the pictures glow:
The good of life is precious to us both.
She cannot love; what do I want with rule?
When first I saw your face a year ago
I knew my life's good, my soul heard one voice—
"The woman yonder, there 's no use of life
But just to obtain her! heap earth's woes in one
And bear them—make a pile of all earth's joys
And spurn them, as they help or help not this;
Only, obtain her!" How was it to be?
I found you were the cousin of the Queen;
I must then serve the Queen to get to you.
No other way. Suppose there had been one,
And I, by saying prayers to some white star
With promise of my body and my soul,
Might gain you,—should I pray the star or no?
Instead, there was the Queen to serve! I served,
Helped, did what other servants failed to do.
Neither she sought nor I declared my end.
Her good is hers, my recompense be mine,—
I therefore name you as that recompense.
She dreamed that such a thing could never be?
Let her wake now. She thinks there was more cause
In love of power, high fame, pure loyalty?
Perhaps she fancies men wear out their lives
Chasing such shades. Then, I 've a fancy too;
I worked because I want you with my soul:
I therefore ask your hand. Let it be now!

CONSTANCE
Had I not loved you from the very first,
Were I not yours, could we not steal out thus
So wickedly, so wildly, and so well,
You might become impatient. What 's conceived
Of us without here, by the folk within?
Where are you now? immersed in cares of state—
Where am I now? intent on festal robes—
We two, embracing under death's spread hand!
What was this thought for, what that scruple of yours
Which broke the council up?—to bring about

One minute's meeting in the corridor!
And then the sudden sleights, strange secrecies,
Complots inscrutable, deep telegraphs,
Long-planned chance-meetings, hazards of a look,
"Does she know? does she not know? saved or lost?"
A year of this compression's ecstasy
All goes for nothing! you would give this up
For the old way, the open way, the world's,
His way who beats, and his who sells his wife!
What tempts you?—their notorious happiness
Makes you ashamed of ours? The best you 'll gain
Will be—the Queen grants all that you require,
Concedes the cousin, rids herself of you
And me at once, and gives us ample leave
To live like our five hundred happy friends.
The world will show us with officious hand
Our chamber-entry, and stand sentinel
Where we so oft have stolen across its traps!
Get the world's warrant, ring the falcons' feet,
And make it duty to be bold and swift,
Which long ago was nature. Have it so!
We never hawked by rights till flung from fist?
Oh, the man's thought! no woman's such a fool.

NORBERT

Yes, the man's thought and my thought, which is more—
One made to love you, let the world take note!
Have I done worthy work? be love's the praise,
Though hampered by restrictions, barred against
By set forms, blinded by forced secrecies!
Set free my love, and see what love can do
Shown in my life—what work will spring from that!
The world is used to have its business done
On other grounds, find great effects produced
For power's sake, fame's sake, motives in men's mouth.
So, good: but let my low ground shame their high!
Truth is the strong thing. Let man's life be true!
And love's the truth of mine. Time prove the rest!
I choose to wear you stamped all over me,
Your name upon my forehead and my breast,
You, from the sword's blade to the ribbon's edge,
That men may see, all over, you in me—
That pale loves may die out of their pretence
In face of mine, shames thrown on love fall off.
Permit this, Constance! Love has been so long
Subdued in me, eating me through and through,
That now 't is all of me and must have way.
Think of my work, that chaos of intrigues,

Those hopes and fears, surprises and delays,
That long endeavor, earnest, patient, slow,
Trembling at last to its assured result:
Then think of this revulsion! I resume
Life after death, (it is no less than life,
After such long unlovely laboring days,)
And liberate to beauty life's great need
O' the beautiful, which, while it prompted work,
Suppressed itself erewhile. This eve's the time,
This eve intense with yon first trembling star
We seem to pant and reach; scarce aught between
The earth that rises and the heaven that bends;
All nature self-abandoned, every tree
Flung as it will, pursuing its own thoughts
And fixed so, every flower and every weed,
No pride, no shame, no victory, no defeat;
All under God, each measured by itself.
These statues round us stand abrupt, distinct,
The strong in strength, the weak in weakness fixed,
The Muse forever wedded to her lyre,
Nymph to her fawn, and Silence to her rose:
See God's approval on his universe!
Let us do so—aspire to live as these
In harmony with truth, ourselves being true!
Take the first way, and let the second come!
My first is to possess myself of you;
The music sets the march-step—forward, then!
And there 's the Queen, I go to claim you of,
The world to witness, wonder and applaud.
Our flower of life breaks open. No delay!

CONSTANCE
And so shall we be ruined, both of us.
Norbert, I know her to the skin and bone:
You do not know her, were not born to it,
To feel what she can see or cannot see.
Love, she is generous,—ay, despite your smile,
Generous as you are: for, in that thin frame
Pain-twisted, punctured through and through with cares,
There lived a lavish soul until it starved,
Debarred of healthy food. Look to the soul—
Pity that, stoop to that, ere you begin
(The true man's—way) on justice and your rights,
Exactions and acquittance of the past!
Begin so—see what justice she will deal!
We women hate a debt as men a gift.
Suppose her some poor keeper of a school
Whose business is to sit through summer months

And dole out children leave to go and play,
Herself superior to such lightness—she
In the arm-chair's state and pædagogic pomp—
To the life, the laughter, sun and youth outside:
We wonder such a face looks black on us?
I do not bid you wake her tenderness,
(That were vain truly—none is left to wake,)
But, let her think her justice is engaged
To take the shape of tenderness, and mark
If she 'll not coldly pay its warmest debt!
Does she love me, I ask you? not a whit:
Yet, thinking that her justice was engaged
To help a kinswoman, she took me up—
Did more on that bare ground than other loves
Would do on greater argument. For me,
I have no equivalent of such cold kind
To pay her with, but love alone to give
If I give anything. I give her love:
I feel I ought to help her, and I will.
So, for her sake, as yours, I tell you twice
That women hate a debt as men a gift.
If I were you, I could obtain this grace—
Could lay the whole I did to love's account,
Nor yet be very false as courtiers go—
Declaring my success was recompense;
It would be so, in fact: what were it else?
And then, once loose her generosity,—
Oh, how I see it! then, were I but you
To turn it, let it seem to move itself,
And make it offer what I really take,
Accepting just, in the poor cousin's hand,
Her value as the next thing to the Queen's—
Since none love Queens directly, none dare that,
And a thing's shadow or a name's mere echo
Suffices those who miss the name and thing!
You pick up just a ribbon she has worn,
To keep in proof how near her breath you came.
Say, I 'm so near I seem a piece of her—
Ask for me that way—(oh, you understand,)
You 'd find the same gift yielded with a grace,
Which, if you make the least show to extort ...
—You 'll see! and when you have ruined both of us,
Dissertate on the Queen's ingratitude!

NORBERT
Then, if I turn it that way, you consent?
'T is not my way; I have more hope in truth:
Still, if you won't have truth—why, this indeed,

Were scarcely false, as I 'd express the sense.
Will you remain here?

CONSTANCE
O best heart of mine,
How I have loved you! then, you take my way?
Are mine as you have been her minister,
Work out my thought, give it effect for me,
Paint plain my poor conceit and make it serve?
I owe that withered woman everything—
Life, fortune, you, remember! Take my part—
Help me to pay her! Stand upon your rights?
You, with my rose, my hands, my heart on you?
Your rights are mine—you have no rights but mine.

NORBERT
Remain here. How you know me!

CONSTANCE
Ah, but still—

[He breaks from her; she remains. Dance-music from within.

[Enter the **QUEEN**.

QUEEN
Constance? She is here as he said. Speak quick!
Is it so? Is it true or false? One word!

CONSTANCE
True.

QUEEN
Mercifullest Mother, thanks to thee!

CONSTANCE
Madam?

QUEEN
I love you, Constance, from my soul.
Now say once more, with any words you will,
'T is true, all true, as true as that I speak.

CONSTANCE
Why should you doubt it?

QUEEN
Ah, why doubt? why doubt?

Dear, make me see it! Do you see it so?
None see themselves; another sees them best.
You say "why doubt it?"—you see him and me.
It is because the Mother has such grace
That if we had but faith—wherein we fail—
Whate'er we yearn for would be granted us;
Yet still we let our whims prescribe despair,
Our fancies thwart and cramp our will and power,
And while accepting life, abjure its use.
Constance, I had abjured the hope of love
And being loved, as truly as yon palm
The hope of seeing Egypt from that plot.

CONSTANCE
Heaven!

QUEEN
But it was so, Constance, it was so!
Men say—or do men say it? fancies say—
"Stop here, your life is set, you are grown old.
Too late—no love for you, too late for love—
Leave love to girls. Be queen: let Constance love!"
One takes the hint—half meets it like a child,
Ashamed at any feelings that oppose.
"Oh love, true, never think of love again!
I am a queen: I rule, not love, forsooth."
So it goes on; so a face grows like this,
Hair like this hair, poor arms as lean as these,
Till,—nay, it does not end so, I thank God!

CONSTANCE
I cannot understand—

QUEEN
The happier you!
Constance, I know not how it is with men:
For women (I am a woman now like you)
There is no good of life but love—but love!
What else looks good, is some shade flung from love;
Love gilds it, gives it worth. Be warned by me,
Never you cheat yourself one instant! Love,
Give love, ask only love, and leave the rest!
O Constance, how I love you!

CONSTANCE
I love you.

QUEEN

I do believe that all is come through you.
I took you to my heart to keep it warm
When the last chance of love seemed dead in me;
I thought your fresh youth warmed my withered heart.
Oh, I am very old now, am I not?
Not so! it is true and it shall be true!

CONSTANCE
Tell it me: let me judge if true or false.

QUEEN
Ah, but I fear you! you will look at me
And say, "she 's old, she 's grown unlovely quite
Who ne'er was beauteous: men want beauty still."
Well, so I feared—the curse! so I felt sure!

CONSTANCE
Be calm. And now you feel not sure, you say?

QUEEN
Constance, he came,—the coming was not strange—
Do not I stand and see men come and go?
I turned a half-look from my pedestal
Where I grow marble—"one young man the more!
He will love some one; that is naught to me:
What would he with my marble stateliness?"
Yet this seemed somewhat worse than heretofore;
The man more gracious, youthful, like a god,
And I still older, with less flesh to change—
We two those dear extremes that long to touch.
It seemed still harder when he first began
To labor at those state-affairs, absorbed
The old way for the old end—interest.
Oh, to live with a thousand beating hearts
Around you, swift eyes, serviceable hands,
Professing they 've no care but for your cause,
Thought but to help you, love but for yourself,—
And you the marble statue all the time
They praise and point at as preferred to life,
Yet leave for the first breathing woman's smile,
First dancer's, gypsy's, or street baladine's!
Why, how I have ground my teeth to hear men's speech
Stifled for fear it should alarm my ear,
Their gait subdued lest step should startle me,
Their eyes declined, such queendom to respect,
Their hands alert, such treasure to preserve,
While not a man of them broke rank and spoke,
Wrote me a vulgar letter all of love.

Or caught my hand and pressed it like a hand!
There have been moments, if the sentinel
Lowering his halbert to salute the queen,
Had flung it brutally and clasped my knees,
I would have stooped and kissed him with my soul.

CONSTANCE
Who could have comprehended?

QUEEN
Ay, who—who?
Why, no one, Constance, but this one who did.
Not they, not you, not I. Even now perhaps
It comes too late—would you but tell the truth.

CONSTANCE
I wait to tell it.

QUEEN
Well, you see, he came,
Outfaced the others, did a work this year
Exceeds in value all was ever done,
You know—it is not I who say it—all
Say it. And so (a second pang and worse)
I grew aware not only of what he did,
But why so wondrously. Oh, never work
Like his was done for work's ignoble sake—
Souls need a finer aim to light and lure!
I felt, I saw, he loved—loved somebody.
And Constance, my dear Constance, do you know,
I did believe this while 't was you he loved.

CONSTANCE
Me, madam?

QUEEN
It did seem to me, your face
Met him where'er he looked: and whom but you
Was such a man to love? It seemed to me,
You saw he loved you, and approved his love,
And both of you were in intelligence.
You could not loiter in that garden, step
Into this balcony, but I straight was stung
And forced to understand. It seemed so true,
So right, so beautiful, so like you both,
That all this work should have been done by him
Not for the vulgar hope of recompense,
But that at last—suppose, some night like this—

Borne on to claim his due reward of me,
He might say, "Give her hand and pay me so."
And I (O Constance, you shall love me now!)
I thought, surmounting all the bitterness,
—"And he shall have it. I will make her blest,
My flower of youth, my woman's self that was,
My happiest woman's self that might have been!
These two shall have their joy and leave me here."
Yes—yes!

CONSTANCE
Thanks!

QUEEN
And the word was on my lips
When he burst in upon me. I looked to hear
A mere calm statement of his just desire
For payment of his labor. When—O heaven,
How can I tell you? lightning on my eyes
And thunder in my ears proved that first word
Which told 't was love of me, of me, did all—
He loved me—from the first step to the last,
Loved me!

CONSTANCE
You hardly saw, scarce heard him speak
Of love: what if you should mistake?

QUEEN
No, no—
No mistake! Ha, there shall be no mistake!
He had not dared to hint the love he felt—
You were my reflex—(how I understood!)
He said you were the ribbon I had worn,
He kissed my hand, he looked into my eyes,
And love, love came at end of every phrase.
Love is begun; this much is come to pass:
The rest is easy. Constance, I am yours!
I will learn, I will place my life on you,
Teach me but how to keep what I have won!
Am I so old? This hair was early gray;
But joy ere now has brought hair brown again,
And joy will bring the cheek's red back, I feel.
I could sing once too; that was in my youth.
Still, when men paint me, they declare me ... yes,
Beautiful—for the last French painter did!
I know they flatter somewhat; you are frank—
I trust you. How I loved you from the first!

Some queens would hardly seek a cousin out
And set her by their side to take the eye:
I must have felt that good would come from you.
I am not generous—like him—like you!
But he is not your lover after all:
It was not you he looked at. Saw you him?
You have not been mistaking words or looks?
He said you were the reflex of myself.
And yet he is not such a paragon
To you, to younger women who may choose
Among a thousand Norberts. Speak the truth!
You know you never named his name to me:
You know, I cannot give him up—ah God,
Not up now, even to you!

CONSTANCE
Then calm yourself.

QUEEN
See, I am old—look here, you happy girl!
I will not play the fool, deceive—ah, whom?
'T is all gone: put your cheek beside my cheek
And what a contrast does the moon behold!
But then I set my life upon one chance,
The last chance and the best—am I not left,
My soul, myself? All women love great men
If young or old; it is in all the tales:
Young beauties love old poets who can love—
Why should not he, the poems in my soul,
The passionate faith, the pride of sacrifice,
Life-long, death-long? I throw them at his feet.
Who cares to see the fountain's very shape,
Whether it be a Triton's or a Nymph's
That pours the foam, makes rainbows all around?
You could not praise indeed the empty conch;
But I 'll pour floods of love and hide myself.
How I will love him! Cannot men love love?
Who was a queen and loved a poet once
Humpbacked, a dwarf? ah, women can do that!
Well, but men too; at least, they tell you so.
They love so many women in their youth,
And even in age they all love whom they please;
And yet the best of them confide to friends
That 't is not beauty makes the lasting love—
They spend a day with such and tire the next:
They like soul,—well then, they like phantasy,
Novelty even. Let us confess the truth,
Horrible though it be, that prejudice,

Prescription ... curses! they will love a queen.
They will, they do: and will not, does not—he?

CONSTANCE
How can he? You are wedded: 't is a name
We know, but still a bond. Your rank remains,
His rank remains. How can he, nobly souled
As you believe and I incline to think,
Aspire to be your favorite, shame and all?

QUEEN
Hear her! There, there now—could she love like me?
What did I say of smooth-cheeked youth and grace?
See all it does or could do! so youth loves!
Oh, tell him, Constance, you could never do
What I will—you, it was not born in! I
Will drive these difficulties far and fast
As yonder mists curdling before the moon.
I 'll use my light too, gloriously retrieve
My youth from its enforced calamity,
Dissolve that hateful marriage, and be his,
His own in the eyes alike of God and man.

CONSTANCE
You will do—dare do ... pause on what you say!

QUEEN
Hear her! I thank you, sweet, for that surprise.
You have the fair face: for the soul, see mine!
I have the strong soul: let me teach you, here.
I think I have borne enough and long enough,
And patiently enough, the world remarks,
To have my own way now, unblamed by all.
It does so happen (I rejoice for it)
This most unhoped-for issue cuts the knot.
There 's not a better way of settling claims
Than this; God sends the accident express:
And were it for my subjects' good, no more,
'T were best thus ordered. I am thankful now,
Mute, passive, acquiescent. I receive,
And bless God simply, or should almost fear
To walk so smoothly to my ends at last.
Why, how I baffle obstacles, spurn fate!
How strong I am! Could Norbert see me now!

CONSTANCE
Let me consider. It is all too strange.

QUEEN

You, Constance, learn of me; do you, like me!
You are young, beautiful: my own, best girl,
You will have many lovers, and love one—
Light hair, not hair like Norbert's, to suit yours,
Taller than he is, since yourself are tall.
Love him, like me! Give all away to him;
Think never of yourself; throw by your pride,
Hope, fear,—your own good as you saw it once,
And love him simply for his very self.
Remember, I (and what am I to you?)
Would give up all for one, leave throne, lose life.
Do all but just unlove him! He loves me.

CONSTANCE

He shall.

QUEEN

You, step inside my inmost heart!
Give me your own heart: let us have one heart!
I 'll come to you for counsel; "this he says,
This he does; what should this amount to, pray?
Beseech you, change it into current coin!
Is that worth kisses? Shall I please him there?"
And then we 'll speak in turn of you—what else?
Your love, according to your beauty's worth,
For you shall have some noble love, all gold:
Whom choose you? we will get him at your choice.
—Constance, I leave you. Just a minute since,
I felt as I must die or be alone
Breathing my soul into an ear like yours:
Now, I would face the world with my new life,
Wear my new crown. I 'll walk around the rooms,
And then come back and tell you how it feels.
How soon a smile of God can change the world!
How we are made for happiness—how work
Grows play, adversity a winning fight!
True, I have lost so many years: what then?
Many remain: God has been very good.
You, stay here! 'T is as different from dreams,
From the mind's cold calm estimate of bliss,
As these stone statues from the flesh and blood.
The comfort thou hast caused mankind, God's moon!

[She goes out, leaving **CONSTANCE**. Dance-music from within.

[**NORBERT** enters.

NORBERT
Well? we have but one minute and one word!

CONSTANCE
I am yours, Norbert!

NORBERT
Yes, mine.

CONSTANCE
Not till now!
You were mine. Now I give myself to you.

NORBERT
Constance?

CONSTANCE
Your own! I know the thriftier way
Of giving—haply, 't is the wiser way.
Meaning to give a treasure, I might dole
Coin after coin out (each, as that were all,
With a new largess still at each despair)
And force you keep in sight the deed, preserve
Exhaustless till the end my part and yours,
My giving and your taking; both our joys
Dying together. Is it the wiser way?
I choose the simpler; I give all at once.
Know what you have to trust to, trade upon!
Use it, abuse it,—anything but think
Hereafter, "Had I known she loved me so,
And what my means, I might have thriven with it."
This is your means. I give you all myself.

NORBERT
I take you and thank God.

CONSTANCE
Look on through years!
We cannot kiss, a second day like this;
Else were this earth no earth.

NORBERT
With this day's heat
We shall go on through years of cold.

CONSTANCE
So, best!
—I try to see those years—I think I see.

You walk quick and new warmth comes; you look back
And lay all to the first glow—not sit down
Forever brooding on a day like this
While seeing embers whiten and love die.
Yes, love lives best in its effect; and mine,
Full in its own life, yearns to live in yours.

NORBERT
Just so. I take and know you all at once.
Your soul is disengaged so easily.
Your face is there, I know you; give me time,
Let me be proud and think you shall know me.
My soul is slower: in a life I roll
The minute out whereto you condense yours—
The whole slow circle round you I must move,
To be just you. I look to a long life
To decompose this minute, prove its worth.
'T is the sparks' long succession one by one
Shall show you, in the end, what fire was crammed
In that mere stone you struck: how could you know,
If it lay ever unproved in your sight,
As now my heart lies? your own warmth would hide
Its coldness, were it cold.

CONSTANCE
But how prove, how?

NORBERT
Prove in my life, you ask?

CONSTANCE
Quick, Norbert—how?

NORBERT
That 's easy told. I count life just a stuff
To try the soul's strength on, educe the man.
Who keeps one end in view makes all things serve
As with the body—he who hurls a lance
Or heaps up stone on stone, shows strength alike:
So must I seize and task all means to prove
And show this soul of mine, you crown as yours,
And justify us both.

CONSTANCE
Could you write books,
Paint pictures! One sits down in poverty
And writes or paints, with pity for the rich.

NORBERT

And loves one's painting and one's writing, then.
And not one's mistress! All is best, believe,
And we best as no other than we are.
We live, and they experiment on life—
Those poets, painters, all who stand aloof
To overlook the farther. Let us be
The thing they look at! I might take your face
And write of it and paint it—to what end?
For whom? what pale dictatress in the air
Feeds, smiling sadly, her fine ghost-like form
With earth's real blood and breath, the beauteous life
She makes despised forever? You are mine,
Made for me, not for others in the world,
Nor yet for that which I should call my art,
The cold calm power to see how fair you look.
I come to you; I leave you not, to write
Or paint. You are, I am: let Rubens there
Paint us!

CONSTANCE

So, best!

NORBERT

I understand your soul,
You live, and rightly sympathize with life,
With action, power, success. This way is straight;
And time were short, beside, to let me change
The craft my childhood learnt: my craft shall serve.
Men set me here to subjugate, enclose,
Manure their barren lives, and force thence fruit
First for themselves, and afterward for me
In the due tithe; the task of some one soul,
Through ways of work appointed by the world.
I am not bid create—men see no star
Transfiguring my brow to warrant that—
But find and bind and bring to bear their wills.
So I began: to-night sees how I end.
What if it see, too, power's first outbreak here
Amid the warmth, surprise and sympathy,
And instincts of the heart that teach the head?
What if the people have discerned at length
The dawn of the next nature, novel brain
Whose will they venture in the place of theirs,
Whose work, they trust, shall find them as novel ways
To untried heights which yet he only sees?
I felt it when you kissed me. See this Queen,
This people—in our phrase this mass of men—

See how the mass lies passive to my hand
Now that my hand is plastic, with you by
To make the muscles iron! Oh, an end
Shall crown this issue as this crowns the first!
My will be on the people! then, the strain,
The grappling of the potter with his clay,
The long uncertain struggle,—the success
And consummation of the spirit-work,
Some vase shape to the curl of the god's lip,
While rounded fair for human sense to see
The Graces in a dance men recognize
With turbulent applause and laughs of heart!
So triumph ever shall renew itself;
Ever shall end in efforts higher yet,
Ever begin ...

CONSTANCE
I ever helping?

NORBERT
Thus!

[As he embraces her, the **QUEEN** enters.

CONSTANCE
Hist, madam! So have I performed my part.
You see your gratitude's true decency,
Norbert? A little slow in seeing it!
Begin, to end the sooner! What 's a kiss?

NORBERT
Constance?

CONSTANCE
Why, must I teach it you again?
You want a witness to your dulness, sir?
What was I saying these ten minutes long?
Then I repeat—when some young handsome man
Like you has acted out a part like yours,
Is pleased to fall in love with one beyond,
So very far beyond him, as he says—
So hopelessly in love that but to speak
Would prove him mad,—he thinks judiciously,
And makes some insignificant good soul,
Like me, his friend, adviser, confidant,
And very stalking-horse to cover him
In following after what he dares not face—
When his end 's gained—(sir, do you understand)

When she, he dares not face, has loved him first,
—May I not say so, madam?—tops his hope,
And overpasses so his wildest dream,
With glad consent of all, and most of her
The confidant who brought the same about—
Why, in the moment when such joy explodes,
I do hold that the merest gentleman
Will not start rudely from the stalking-horse,
Dismiss it with a "There, enough of you!"
Forget it, show his back unmannerly;
But like a liberal heart will rather turn
And say, "A tingling time of hope was ours;
Betwixt the fears and falterings, we two lived
A chanceful time in waiting for the prize:
The confidant, the Constance, served not ill.
And though I shall forget her in good time,
Her use being answered now, as reason bids,
Nay as herself bids from her heart of hearts,—
Still, she has rights, the first thanks go to her,
The first good praise goes to the prosperous tool,
And the first—which is the last—rewarding kiss."

NORBERT
Constance, it is a dream—ah, see, you smile!

CONSTANCE
So, now his part being properly performed,
Madam, I turn to you and finish mine
As duly; I do justice in my turn.
Yes, madam, he has loved you—long and well;
He could not hope to tell you so—'t was I
Who served to prove your soul accessible,
I led his thoughts on, drew them to their place
When they had wandered else into despair,
And kept love constant toward its natural aim.
Enough, my part is played; you stoop half-way
And meet us royally and spare our fears:
'T is like yourself. He thanks you, so do I.
Take him—with my full heart! my work is praised
By what comes of it. Be you happy, both!
Yourself—the only one on earth who can—
Do all for him, much more than a mere heart
Which though warm is not useful in its warmth
As the silk vesture of a queen! fold that
Around him gently, tenderly. For him—
For him,—he knows his own part!

NORBERT

Have you done?
I take the jest at last. Should I speak now?
Was yours the wager, Constance, foolish child,
Or did you but accept it? Well—at least
You lose by it.

CONSTANCE
Nay, madam, 't is your turn!
Restrain him still from speech a little more,
And make him happier as more confident!
Pity him, madam, he is timid yet!
Mark, Norbert! Do not shrink now! Here I yield
My whole right in you to the Queen, observe!
With her go put in practice the great schemes
You teem with, follow the career else closed—
Be all you cannot be except by her!
Behold her!—Madam, say for pity's sake
Anything—frankly say you love him! Else
He 'll not believe it: there 's more earnest in
His fear than you conceive: I know the man!

NORBERT
I know the woman somewhat, and confess
I thought she had jested better: she begins
To overcharge her part. I gravely wait
Your pleasure, madam: where is my reward?

QUEEN
Norbert, this wild girl (whom I recognize
Scarce more than you do, in her fancy-fit,
Eccentric speech and variable mirth,
Not very wise perhaps and somewhat bold,
Yet suitable, the whole night's work being strange)
—May still be right: I may do well to speak
And make authentic what appears a dream
To even myself. For, what she says is true:
Yes, Norbert—what you spoke just now of love,
Devotion, stirred no novel sense in me,
But justified a warmth felt long before.
Yes, from the first—I loved you, I shall say:
Strange! but I do grow stronger, now 't is said.
Your courage helps mine: you did well to speak
To-night, the night that crowns your twelve-months' toil:
But still I had not waited to discern
Your heart so long, believe me! From the first
The source of so much zeal was almost plain,
In absence even of your own words just now
Which hazarded the truth. 'T is very strange,

But takes a happy ending—in your love
Which mine meets: be it so! as you choose me,
So I choose you.

NORBERT
And worthily you choose.
I will not be unworthy your esteem,
No, madam. I do love you; I will meet
Your nature, now I know it. This was well.
I see,—you dare and you are justified:
But none had ventured such experiment,
Less versed than you in nobleness of heart,
Less confident of finding such in me.
I joy that thus you test me ere you grant
The dearest, richest, beauteousest and best
Of women to my arms: 't is like yourself.
So—back again into my part 's set words—
Devotion to the uttermost is yours,
But no, you cannot, madam, even you,
Create in me the love our Constance does.
Or—something truer to the tragic phrase—
Not yon magnolia-bell superb with scent
Invites a certain insect—that 's myself—
But the small eye-flower nearer to the ground.
I take this lady.

CONSTANCE
Stay—not hers, the trap—
Stay, Norbert—that mistake were worst of all!
He is too cunning, madam! It was I,
I, Norbert, who ...

NORBERT
You, was it, Constance? Then,
But for the grace of this divinest hour
Which gives me you, I might not pardon here!
I am the Queen's; she only knows my brain:
She may experiment upon my heart
And I instruct her too by the result.
But you, Sweet, you who know me, who so long
Have told my heartbeats over, held my life
In those white hands of yours,—it is not well!

CONSTANCE
Tush! I have said it, did I not say it all?
The life, for her—the heartbeats, for her sake!

NORBERT

Enough! my cheek grows red, I think. Your test?
There 's not the meanest woman in the world,
Not she I least could love in all the world,
Whom, did she love me, had love proved itself,
I dare insult as you insult me now.
Constance, I could say, if it must be said,
"Take back the soul you offer, I keep mine!"
But—"Take the soul still quivering on your hand,
The soul so offered, which I cannot use,
And, please you, give it to some playful friend,
For—what 's the trifle he requites me with?"
I, tempt a woman, to amuse a man.
That two may mock her heart if it succumb?
No: fearing God and standing 'neath his heaven,
I would not dare insult a woman so,
Were she the meanest woman in the world,
And he, I cared to please, ten emperors!

CONSTANCE
Norbert!

NORBERT
I love once as I live but once.
What case is this to think or talk about?
I love you. Would it mend the case at all
If such a step as this killed love in me?
Your part were done: account to God for it!
But mine—could murdered love get up again,
And kneel to whom you please to designate,
And make you mirth? It is too horrible.
You did not know this, Constance? now you know
That body and soul have each one life, but one:
And here 's my love, here, living, at your feet.

CONSTANCE
See the Queen! Norbert—this one more last word—
If thus you have taken jest for earnest—thus
Loved me in earnest ...

NORBERT
Ah, no jest holds here!
Where is the laughter in which jests break up,
And what this horror that grows palpable?
Madam—why grasp you thus the balcony?
Have I done ill? Have I not spoken truth?
How could I other? Was it not your test,
To try me, what my love for Constance meant?
Madam, your royal soul itself approves,

The first, that I should choose thus! so one takes
A beggar,—asks him, what would buy his child?
And then approves the expected laugh of scorn
Returned as something noble from the rags.
Speak, Constance, I 'm the beggar! Ha, what 's this?
You two glare each at each like panthers now.
Constance, the world fades; only you stand there!
You did not, in to-night's wild whirl of things,
Sell me—your soul of souls, for any price?
No—no—'t is easy to believe in you!
Was it your love's mad trial to o'ertop
Mine by this vain self-sacrifice? well, still—
Though I might curse, I love you. I am love
And cannot change: love's self is at your feet!

[The **QUEEN** goes out.

CONSTANCE
Feel my heart; let it die against your own!

NORBERT
Against my own. Explain not; let this be!
This is life's height.

CONSTANCE
Yours, yours, yours!

NORBERT
You and I—
Why care by what meanders we are here
I' the centre of the labyrinth? Men have died
Trying to find this place, which we have found.

CONSTANCE
Found, found!

NORBERT
Sweet, never fear what she can do!
We are past harm now.

CONSTANCE
On the breast of God.
I thought of men—as if you were a man.
Tempting him with a crown!

NORBERT
This must end here:
It is too perfect.

CONSTANCE
There 's the music stopped.
What measured heavy tread? It is one blaze
About me and within me.

NORBERT
Oh, some death
Will run its sudden finger round this spark
And sever us from the rest!

CONSTANCE
And so do well.
Now the doors open.

NORBERT
'T is the guard comes.

CONSTANCE
Kiss!

Robert Browning – A Short Biography

He is the equal of any Victorian Poet that could be mentioned. However, Browning continues to be in the shadow of Tennyson, Arnold, Hopkins, Morris and many others.

Robert Browning was born on May 7th, 1812 in Walworth in the parish of Camberwell, London. He was baptized on June 14th, 1812, at Lock's Fields Independent Chapel, York Street, Walworth.

Browning's early years were certainly very interesting. His mother was an excellent pianist and a very devout evangelical Christian. His father, who worked as a clerk at the Bank of England, was also an artist, scholar, antiquarian, and collector of books and pictures. Indeed, he amassed more than 6,000 volumes of rare books including works in Greek, Hebrew, Latin, French, Italian, and Spanish. For the young and curious Browning, it was a wonderful resource, added to which his father was a guiding force in his education.

Many accounts attest that Browning was already proficient at reading and writing by the age of five. He is said to have been a bright but anxious student and to have studied and learnt Latin, Greek, and French by the time he was fourteen. From fourteen to sixteen he was educated at home, tutored in music, drawing, dancing, and horsemanship. Certainly, language and the arts were two areas the young Browning both absorbed and pushed himself towards.

At the age of twelve he wrote a volume of Byronic verse he called Incondita, which his parents attempted to have published. The attempts were unsuccessful and, disappointed, Browning destroyed the work.

In 1825, a cousin gave Browning a collection of Percy Bysshe Shelley's poetry; Browning was so enamored with the poems that he asked for the rest of Shelley's works for his thirteenth birthday. In fact, Browning then went the extra mile, declaring himself to be both a vegetarian and an atheist in honour of his hero.

Intriguingly it seems that the rejection of his first volume didn't dim his appreciation of other poets, but it appears to have stopped him writing any poems between the ages of thirteen and twenty.

In 1828, Browning enrolled at the newly-opened University of London. He was uncomfortable with the experience and he soon left, anxious to read and absorb at his own pace.

His education which, overall is notably rambling and lacks a structure that many of his artistic contemporaries enjoyed, i.e. excellent public schooling and then a degree at Oxford or Cambridge, may present many of his critics with ammunition to criticize, but alternatively his hap-hazard education certainly contributed to many of the references that baffled both critics and his audience, but they tellingly show the breath and scale of what he could turn words too. What others would call obscure references were, to Browning, remarkably obvious.

Browning's early career was very promising. His long poem Pauline (of which only a fragment was ever finished and published) brought him to the attention of the Pre-Raphaelite master Dante Gabriel Rossetti and his difficult Paracelsus (published in 1835) was warmly admired by both Dickens and Wordsworth.

In the 1830s he met the actor William Macready and was encouraged to develop and turn his talents to the stage by writing verse drama. But these plays, including Strafford, which ran for five nights in 1837, and those contained within the Bells and Pomegranates series, were, for the most part, unsuccessful.

During this period Browning began to discover that his real talents lay in taking a single character and allowing that character to discover more about himself by revealing further personal aspects of himself in his speeches; the dramatic monologue. The techniques he developed through this—especially the use of diction, rhythm, and symbol—are regarded as his most important contribution to poetry. They would later influence such major poets of the 20th Century as Ezra Pound, T. S. Eliot, and Robert Frost.

By 1840, with the publication of Sordello, the tide turned somewhat. Many thought he was being deliberately obscure, opaque beyond measure and his poetry for the next decade or so was not eagerly acquired or talked about.

As Browning attempted to rehabilitate his career he began a relationship with Elizabeth Barrett in 1845. He had read her poems and, being totally charmed by their quality, was determined to meet her. The poetess was better known than the younger Browning but suffered from a debilitating illness and was also subject to the harsh behaviour of her over-bearing father. Nevertheless, the new couple were soon inseparable.

Her father, as he did with any of his children that married, disinherited her. Despite this she had some money from her own resources and sensing that the best outcome for both the relationship and her own health was to move abroad the couple did just that. After a private marriage at St Marylebone Parish Church, in September 1846, they journeyed to Europe to honeymoon in Paris.

Their new life now took them to Italy, first to Pisa and a little later to Florence. There they absorbed life and one another.

But in the short term the literary assault on Browning's work did not let up. He was now criticized by such patrician writers as Charles Kingsley for his abandonment of England for foreign lands. Browning could do little to answer these attacks except to compose with his pen and continue with his poetical journey.

The Browning's were well respected, and even famous. Elizabeth health began to improve, she grew stronger and in 1849, at the age of 43, between four miscarriages, she gave birth to a son, Robert Wiedeman Barrett Browning, whom they nicknamed "Penini" or "Pen",

Intriguingly despite his growing reputation and return to form as a poet he was more often than not known as 'Elizabeth Barrett's husband'.

Work flowed from his pen that was to ensure his reputation as one of England's leading poets. When his collection Men and Women was published in 1855 it contained some of his finest lines. It was dedicated to Elizabeth. Life had begun to smile handsome rewards upon the Brownings.

Victorian society was very much taken with all things spiritualist. It was not enough to have command of much of the globe through Empire, they wished to know and explore wherever they could. The spirit world beckoned their interest. Browning dissented from this view believing it was all a hoax and a fraud. Elizabeth, however, was inclined to believe and this caused several disagreements between the couple.

They attended a séance by Daniel Dunglas Home, in July 1855. (Home was a famous and clamored after Scottish physical medium with the reported ability to levitate and speak with the dead). It is said that during this séance a spirit face materialised. Home then claimed it was the face of Browning's son who had died in infancy. Browning seized the 'materialisation' which turned out to be Home's bare foot. Browning had never lost a son in infancy.

After the séance, Browning wrote an angry letter to The Times, in which he said: "the whole display of hands, spirit utterances etc., was a cheat and imposture."

The Browning's time in Italy were immensely rewarding years for both their personal and professional lives. Browning encouraged her to include Sonnets from the Portuguese in her published works, these beautiful poems are undoubtedly one of the highlights of English love poetry.

Elizabeth had become quite politicised during these years. Engrossed in Italian politics (which was continuing to slowly re-unify the country), she issued a small volume of political poems entitled Poems before Congress (1860) most of which were written to express her sympathy with the Italian cause after the earlier outbreak of The Second Italian Independence War in 1859. In England they caused uproar. Conservative magazines such as Blackwood's and the Saturday Review labelled her a fanatic. She dedicated the book to her husband.

But in 1861 tragedy struck.

The couple had spent the winter of 1860–61 in Rome when Elizabeth's health deteriorated again and they returned to Florence in early June. However, these turned out to be her final weeks. Only morphine would now still the pain. She died in Browning's arms on June 29th, 1861. Browning said that she died "smilingly, happily, and with a face like a girl's .... Her last word was .... "Beautiful".

Her burial took place in the nearby Protestant English Cemetery of Florence. The local people were deeply saddened, and shops closed their doors in grief and respect.

Browning and their son were obviously devastated. Unable to bear being in Florence without Elizabeth they soon returned to London to live at 19 Warwick Crescent, Maida Vale.

As he re-integrated himself back into the London literary scene he began to finally receive the proper praise, respect and reputation that his works deserved.

Browning went on to publish Dramatis Personæ (1864), and The Ring and the Book (1868–1869). The latter, based on an "old yellow book" which told of a seventeenth-century Italian murder trial, received wide and generous critical acclaim. Although by now he was in the twilight of a long and prolific career, that had achieved some notable ups and downs, he was respected and indeed renowned for his talents and works.

In 1878, he revisited Italy for the first time since Elizabeth's death. He would return there on several further occasions but never to Florence.

Such was the esteem he was held in that The Browning Society was founded in 1881. Although he had never obtained a degree (something that set him apart from many other Victorian poets) he was now awarded honorary degrees from Oxford University in 1882 and then the University of Edinburgh in 1884.

In 1887, Browning produced the major work of his later years, Parleyings with Certain People of Importance in Their Day. Browning now spoke with his own voice as he engaged in a series of dialogues with long-forgotten figures of literary, artistic, and philosophic history. Unfortunately, both the critics and public were completely baffled by this.

On April 7th, 1889 Browning attended a dinner party at the home of his friend, the artist Rudolf Lehmann. The highlight of which was a recording made on a wax cylinder on an Edison cylinder phonograph. On the recording, which still exists, Browning recites part of How They Brought the Good News from Ghent to Aix, and can even be heard apologising when he forgets the words.

The recording was first played in 1890 on the anniversary of his death, at a gathering of his admirers, it was said to be the first time anyone's voice 'had been heard from beyond the grave'.

His last work Asolando: Fancies and Facts (1889), returned to his brief and concise lyric verse that was so popular. It was published on the day of his death on December 12th, 1889, Robert Browning was at his son's home Ca' Rezzonico in Venice.

He was buried in Poets' Corner in Westminster Abbey; his grave lies immediately adjacent to that of Alfred Tennyson.

Among the many who have publicly acknowledged their literary debt to him are Henry James, Oscar Wilde, George Bernard Shaw, G. K. Chesterton, Ezra Pound, Jorge Luis Borges, and Vladimir Nabokov.

Here follows a list of the plays and poetry volumes published during his lifetime. Poems of particular worth are noted from within those volumes.

Pauline: A Fragment of a Confession (1833)
Paracelsus (1835)
Strafford (play) (1837)
Sordello (1840)
Bells and Pomegranates No. I: Pippa Passes (play) (1841)
      The Year's at the Spring
Bells and Pomegranates No. II: King Victor and King Charles (play) (1842)
Bells and Pomegranates No. III: Dramatic Lyrics (1842)
      Porphyria's Lover
      Soliloquy of the Spanish Cloister
      My Last Duchess
      The Pied Piper of Hamelin
      Count Gismond
      Johannes Agricola in Meditation
Bells and Pomegranates No. IV: The Return of the Druses (play) (1843)
Bells and Pomegranates No. V: A Blot in the 'Scutcheon (play) (1843)
Bells and Pomegranates No. VI: Colombe's Birthday (play) (1844)
Bells and Pomegranates No. VII: Dramatic Romances and Lyrics (1845)
      The Laboratory
      How They Brought the Good News from Ghent to Aix
      The Bishop Orders His Tomb at Saint Praxed's Church
      The Lost Leader
      Home Thoughts from Abroad
      Meeting at Night
Bells and Pomegranates No. VIII: Luria and A Soul's Tragedy (plays) (1846)
Christmas-Eve and Easter-Day (1850)
An Essay on Percy Bysshe Shelley (essay) (1852)
Two Poems (1854)
Men and Women (1855)
      Love Among the Ruins
      A Toccata of Galuppi's
      Childe Roland to the Dark Tower Came
      Fra Lippo Lippi
      Andrea Del Sarto
      The Patriot
      The Last Ride Together
      Memorabilia
      Cleon
      How It Strikes a Contemporary
      The Statue and the Bust
      A Grammarian's Funeral

An Epistle Containing the Strange Medical Experience of Karshish, the Arab Physician
Bishop Blougram's Apology
Master Hugues of Saxe-Gotha
By the Fire-side
Dramatis Personae (1864)
Caliban upon Setebos
Rabbi Ben Ezra
Abt Vogler
Mr. Sludge, "The Medium"
Prospice
A Death in the Desert
The Ring and the Book (1868–69)
Balaustion's Adventure (1871)
Prince Hohenstiel-Schwangau, Saviour of Society (1871)
Fifine at the Fair (1872)
Red Cotton Night-Cap Country, or, Turf and Towers (1873)
Aristophanes' Apology (1875)
Thamuris Marching
The Inn Album (1875)
Pacchiarotto, and How He Worked in Distemper (1876)
Numpholeptos
The Agamemnon of Aeschylus (1877)
La Saisiaz and The Two Poets of Croisic (1878)
Dramatic Idylls (1879)
Dramatic Idylls: Second Series (1880)
Pan and Luna
Jocoseria (1883)
Ferishtah's Fancies (1884)
Parleyings with Certain People of Importance in Their Day (1887)
Asolando (1889)
Prologue
Summum Bonum
Bad Dreams III
Flute-Music, with an Accompaniment
Epilogue

www.ingramcontent.com/pod-product-compliance
Lightning Source LLC
Chambersburg PA
CBHW070113070426
42448CB00038B/2631